ANGRY BIRDS™ PLAYGROUND DINOSAURS

A Prehistoric Adventure!

BY JILL ESBAUM

DINOSAUR ART BY FRANCO TEMPESTA

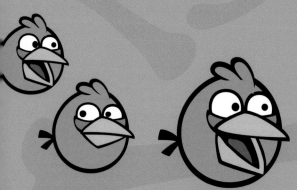

NATIONAL
GEOGRAPHIC

Washington, D.C.

For Gregory — JE

The National Geographic Society is one of the world's largest nonprofit scientific and educational
organizations. Founded in 1888 to "increase and diffuse geographic knowledge," the Society's
mission is to inspire people to care about the planet. It reaches more than 400 million people
worldwide each month through its official journal, *National Geographic,* and other magazines;
National Geographic Channel; television documentaries; music; radio; films; books; DVDs; maps;
exhibitions; live events; school publishing programs; interactive media; and merchandise.
National Geographic has funded more than 10,000 scientific research, conservation and
exploration projects and supports an education program promoting geographic literacy.

For more information, please visit www.nationalgeographic.com,
call 1-800-NGS LINE (647-5463), or write to the following address:
National Geographic Society
1145 17th Street N.W.
Washington, D.C. 20036-4688 U.S.A.

Visit us online at **www.nationalgeographic.com/books**
For librarians and teachers: **www.ngchildrensbooks.org**
More for kids from National Geographic: **kids.nationalgeographic.com**
For information about special discounts for bulk purchases, please contact National Geographic
Books Special Sales: **ngspecsales@ngs.org**
For rights or permissions inquiries, please contact National Geographic Books Subsidiary Rights:
ngbookrights@ngs.org

Hardcover ISBN: 978-1-4263-1324-0
Library Edition ISBN: 978-1-4263-1325-7

Printed in the United States of America
13/CK-CML/2

Contents

9

ANGRY BIRDS IN THE TRIASSIC...

TRIASSIC

THE EARLIEST DINOSAURS APPEARED DURING THE TRIASSIC PERIOD, ABOUT 250 MILLION TO 200 MILLION YEARS AGO...

Back then all of Earth's land was connected. We believe that the climate was hot and dry. There were low-growing plants, but probably no tall trees or ice—not even at the North or South Poles. Dinosaurs were reptiles that lived on land. Some walked on two legs, some on four. Some could run fast, others plodded along. Imagine the Triassic dinosaurs . . .

TRIASSIC
250 MILLION TO 200 MILLION YEARS AGO

JURASSIC
200 MILLION TO 145 MILLION YEARS AGO

COELOPHYSIS
Say it: SEE-low-FIE-sis

TRIASSIC

Coelophysis is one of the oldest dinosaurs yet discovered. Hundreds of its skeletons were found in the same place, so scientists think the animals may have died of thirst while searching for water near a dried-up river or stream. We know there was once water in the area because among the dinosaur bones were found fossilized fish, clams, and crayfish.

Coelophysis had long legs and feet, so it was probably a fast runner. It ate lizards and other small animals.

THAT MAKES ME ANGRY.

HEY, NOBODY'S PROTECTING THOSE EGGS!

BONES FOUND IN: U.S. (ARIZONA AND NEW MEXICO)

ON THE MENU: MEAT

SIZE: LESS THAN 9 FEET (3 METERS) LONG

*

*DINOSAUR SIZE COMPARISONS BASED ON THE HEIGHT OF AN AVERAGE 10-YEAR-OLD.

EORAPTOR
Say it: EE-oh-RAP-tore

TRIASSIC

*E*oraptor had five fingers. That's more than later dinosaurs, which had four, three, or only two. *Eoraptor* ate lizards and small mammals. Skull and leg bones from this dinosaur were first discovered in a desert in Argentina, a South American country. Some believe that when it was first discovered, *Eoraptor* was mistakenly identified as a crocodile!

Scientists who search for and study dinosaur fossils to learn about their lives are called paleontologists.

JUST SAY YOU WANT TO BE A DINOSAUR DIGGER!

I WANT TO BE A PALEO... PALEO...

YOU FORGOT THE WORD ALREADY? IT'S A PANTO...NO, WAIT A MINUTE.

BONES FOUND IN: ARGENTINA

ON THE MENU: MEAT

SIZE: 5 FEET (1.5 METERS) LONG

BONES FOUND IN:
ARGENTINA

ON THE MENU: MEAT

SIZE: 16.5 FEET (5 METERS)
LONG

HERRERASAURUS
Say it: huh-RARE-ah-SORE-us

This dinosaur had hinged jaws. That means it could open its huge mouth extra wide to swallow its prey. If it did want smaller bites, no problem. *Herrerasaurus*'s teeth were notched and sharp, and could easily slice through big chunks of meat.

Herrerasaurus walked on its two hind legs. It had long hands, but it couldn't reach very far because of its short arms. Hands probably weren't very important for snatching a meal, anyway. Not with that big, scary mouth!

AREN'T BUGS VEGETABLES?

NO MEAT FOR ME. I'M A VEGETARIAN.

I SAW YOU EAT A BUG YESTERDAY.

LESSEMSAURUS
Say it: LESS-em-SORE-us

*L*essemsaurus was a sauropod. That's what scientists call dinosaurs with small heads, long necks and tails, and thick middles. Sauropods were too heavy to walk on their hind legs. They needed four sturdy legs under them to stomp slowly along. Other animals would have heard them coming from far away—or felt the ground shake.

Lessemsaurus means "Don Lessem's reptile." Lessem is a popular American writer of children's dinosaur books.

EARTHQUAKE!!!

EARTHQUAKE!!!

EARTHQUAKE!!!

PLATEOSAURUS
Say it: PLAT-ee-oh-SORE-us

Plateosaurus had something many dinosaurs did not: cheeks. That tells scientists that it probably ate and ate, stuffing its cheeks with leaves before taking a break to chew and swallow. This dinosaur was the first one able to reach into trees. Even though it was heavy, it could stand on its hind legs and stretch up to pull in tasty tidbits with its beak-like mouth or clawed hands.

Plateosaurus skeletons have been found all across Europe. They lived in herds and may have migrated north and south with changes in weather, always searching for the best feeding grounds.

DO WE HAVE CHEEKS? QUICK, SAY *AHHH.*

AHHHH...

UM...WHAT IS A CHEEK, ANYWAY? I FORGET.

BONES FOUND IN:
NORTHERN AND CENTRAL
EUROPE

ON THE MENU: PLANTS

SIZE: 23 FEET (7 METERS)
LONG

RIOJASAURUS
Say it: REE-oh-hah-SORE-us

TRIASSIC

Bones from *Riojasaurus*, one the first giant dinosaurs, were first discovered in 1967. It was another heavyweight dino. Small holes in some of *Riojasaurus's* bones made those big bones a bit lighter, making it easier for this dinosaur to move around.

Because *Riojasaurus* had 5 front teeth on top and 24 behind them, scientists think it was a gulper. Food went down fast, without much chewing, then was digested down in the animal's stomach.

REMEMBER THAT THE NEXT TIME I MAKE FRUIT SALAD.

ME, TOO!

I LIKE TO EAT FAST.

DURING THE JURASSIC PERIOD, 200 MILLION TO 145 MILLION YEARS AGO, EARTH'S LAND MASSES BEGAN TO PULL APART...

Seas rose higher, and flooding was common. There were deserts, yes, but other lands were green and growing. The first birds appeared. Dinosaurs grew to enormous sizes. There were more and more kinds of them, too. Try to imagine some of the Jurassic dinosaurs . . .

JURASSIC

TRIASSIC
250 MILLION TO 200 MILLION YEARS AGO

JURASSIC
200 MILLION TO 145 MILLION YEARS AGO

EARLY CRETACEOUS
145 MILLION TO 100 MILLION YEARS AGO

LATE CRETACEOUS
100 MILLION TO 65 MILLION YEARS AGO

25

ALLOSAURUS
Say it: AL-oh-SORE-us

JURASSIC

Allosaurus had eight-inch (20-cm) claws and nearly 70 strong, sharp teeth. Its upper teeth curved inward—the better to hold its prey. Its lower jaw could bend outward—making more room for bigger pieces of meat.

Allosaurus was front heavy, and its long tail helped it balance. If it tripped and crashed forward, those small arms wouldn't have been able to stop it from falling on its face. *Ouch!*

The raised ridge in front of each eye is called a crest. This bony crest may have helped protect the dinosaur's eyes during fights with other animals.

I FALL ON MY FACE ALL THE TIME.

YEAH, LIKE WHEN WE FIGHT THE PIGS.

26

BONES FOUND IN:
U.S. (COLORADO, OKLA-
HOMA, UTAH, WYOMING)

ON THE MENU: PLANTS

SIZE: 70 TO 90 FEET (21.3
TO 27.4 METERS) LONG

APATOSAURUS
Say it: uh-PAT-uh-SORE-us

Apatosaurus was a gigantic plant-eating dinosaur. It was once incorrectly known as *Brontosaurus*. This creature needed a *lot* of food. Its teeth were small, blunt pegs, better for stripping leaves than chewing, so it stripped and swallowed, stripped and swallowed, all day long. When tired, *Apatosaurus* napped standing up.

It took strong legs to hold up a dinosaur like this, which weighed as much as two school buses. *Apatosaurus* couldn't run away from predators, but it did have a weapon: its whip-like tail. Scientists think a well-aimed smack of that tail would send an enemy rolling.

YEAH, OR WE'D BE LITTLE BLUE PANCAKES!

WE'D HAVE TO STAY AWAY FROM THOSE STOMPY FEET.

Scientists wonder: Is *Archaeopteryx* the great-great- (and lots more greats) granddaddy of modern day birds?

ARCHAEOPTERYX
Say it: ARK-ee-OP-turr-icks

This little dinosaur gets scientists excited. Why? Because it could be the link proving that the birds we see flying around our neighborhoods every day are related to dinosaurs. Like birds, *Archaeopteryx* had two wings and feathers. But its long tail was like that of a lizard. Other parts were more dinosaur-like, such as sharp teeth and clawed fingers. It may not have been strong enough to flap its wings and fly like the birds we know. But it could probably climb trees and push off to glide through the air.

IT'S A BIRD!

IT'S A DINOSAUR!

BONES FOUND IN: GERMANY

ON THE MENU: MEAT

SIZE: 1.6 FEET (0.5 METER) LONG

IT'S A BIRDOSAUR!

Brachiosaurus
Say it: BRACK-ee-oh-SORE-us

JURASSIC

Brachiosaurus, one of the biggest known sauropods, was a treetop feeder. It is the only dinosaur yet discovered with longer front legs than back legs. It couldn't run fast, but so what? It could just step over anything that got in its way!

One of these giants weighed about as much as six elephants. Pretty amazing when you learn that the skeletons found so far were of *young* animals, not yet fully grown.

BONES FOUND IN: U.S. (COLORADO) AND AFRICA

ON THE MENU: PLANTS

SIZE: 80 TO 85 FEET (24 TO 26 METERS) LONG

OOH! WISH I COULD SLIDE DOWN THAT LONG NECK!

YEAH, WE COULD FLY OFF AND LAND ON THE PIGS. *SPLAT!*

CAMPTOSAURUS
Say it: CAMP-toe-SORE-us

Camptosaurus had short arms, but because it had hooves on its fingers and toes, scientists think it usually walked on all fours. Its head was long and narrow. It used its beak-like mouth to nip leaves. When a hungry predator closed in, Camptosaurus's only hope was to run for it!

BONES FOUND IN: U.S. (COLORADO, NORTH DAKOTA, WYOMING, UTAH) AND ENGLAND

ON THE MENU: PLANTS

SIZE: 23 FEET (7 METERS) LONG

YOU'RE OUTNUMBERED, BUDDY. RUN!

HE NEEDS WINGS.

34

OR A REALLY BIG SLINGSHOT.

Camptosaurus's name means "flexible lizard."

CRYOLOPHOSAURUS
Say it: CRY-oh-LOW-fo-SORE-us

Antarctica is a cold, mostly ice-covered land at the bottom of the Earth. But back when dinosaurs lived, that land was warm and green. So for a long time, scientists believed dinosaurs could have lived there once. But no bones had yet been found.

The first Antarctic dinosaur discovered was *Antarctopelta,* a Cretaceous ankylosaur, in 1985. Then in 1991 an even older Antarctic dinosaur was discovered. A scientist working close to the South Pole found a dino skull unlike any other. This newly discovered dinosaur was named *Cryolophosaurus.* Surprisingly, it had an odd, fan-like crest growing on top of its head.

BONES FOUND IN: ANTARCTICA

ON THE MENU: MEAT

SIZE: 20 FEET (6.1 METERS) LONG

HEY, MISTER! THERE'S A BUTTERFLY SITTING ON YOUR FACE!

Cryolophosaurus's crest was too delicate to be used for fighting or scratching. Scientists think it may simply have been used to attract other dinosaurs.

37

DIPLODOCUS
Say it: dih-PLOD-uh-kus

*D*iplodocus is the largest dinosaur for which scientists have an entire skeleton. For such a huge beast, its skull was surprisingly small. That tells us that *Diplodocus* had a small brain and was not the smartest dino in the neighborhood.

One toe on each foot had a sturdy thumb claw, probably to use against attackers. Its tail may have helped, too. The tail was extremely long and, when snapped, would have made a loud whip crack to scare away predators like *Allosaurus*.

Its triangular teeth tell us that *Diplodocus* probably grabbed branches in its mouth and yanked, stripping them clean of leaves.

MAYBE OUR EGGS WOULDN'T HAVE BEEN STOLEN IF WE'D HID THEM LIKE THAT!

EGGS IN THE GROUND?

INTERESTING IDEA.

Because *Diplodocus*'s eggs have not been found in nests, scientists think this creature dug holes in the ground and lay their eggs in there, like other sauropods.

BONES FOUND IN: U.S. (COLORADO, MONTANA, UTAH, WYOMING)

ON THE MENU: PLANTS

SIZE: 90 FEET (27.4 METERS) LONG

LOURINHANOSAURUS
Say it: lew-reen-ha-no-SORE-us

JURASSIC

A chicken swallows bits of grit or gravel to help grind up food in its gut. What does that have to do with dinosaurs? Some of them did the same thing. *Lourinhanosaurus,* for example.

When scientists discovered the bones of a young *Lourinhanosaurus* in Portugal, they found gastroliths—polished stones—in its stomach area. Nobody has yet found a skull or teeth from this animal, so scientists cannot be sure what it ate. But because bones that have been found resemble a small *Allosaurus,* they think *Lourinhanosaurus* was a meat-eater, too.

I THINK I HAVE A STONE IN MY GUT RIGHT NOW.

NO, THAT'S JUST THIS MORNING'S BREAKFAST.

BONES FOUND IN: PORTUGAL

ON THE MENU: MEAT

SIZE: 26 FEET (8 METERS) LONG

41

MAMENCHISAURUS
Say it: mah-MEHN-chee-SORE-us

JURASSIC

Another *lonnnnng* sauropod, *Mamenchisaurus*'s neck alone was as long as its body and tail combined. No other living creature has ever had a neck so long. Luckily, the bones inside that neck were lightweight. That would have made it easy for the animal to stand in one spot on its sturdy legs and simply swoop that long neck back and forth to munch low-growing shrubs.

WHAT A NECK! THE BREAKFAST HE ATE ON MONDAY ...

Many dinosaur bones are found by accident. *Mamenchisaurus* bones were first discovered in China by workers building a bridge.

SCUTELLOSAURUS
Say it: skoo-TELL-oh-SORE-us

JURASSIC

Scutellosaurus means "little shield lizard." Like some bigger dinosaurs, the top of this animal's skin was made up of hard, bony plates, like on today's alligators and crocodiles. Scientists call those plates *scutes*. Scutes and armor were most likely used for protection. *Scutellosaurus* is the smallest scute-covered dinosaur yet known. Only two skeletons have been found, and each had hundreds of scutes!

LOOK WHO'S TALKING. YOU DON'T EVEN HAVE ARMS—OR WINGS!

IS IT ME, OR DOES HE HAVE REALLY SHORT ARMS?

BONES FOUND IN:
U.S. (ARIZONA)

ON THE MENU: PLANTS

SIZE: 4 FEET (1.2 METERS)
LONG

BONES FOUND IN: CHINA

ON THE MENU: PLANTS

SIZE: 40 FEET (12 METERS) LONG

SHUNOSAURUS
Say it: SHOO-noh-SORE-us

When scientists examined the *Shunosaurus* skeletons found in central China, they were not surprised to see that this dinosaur had four strong legs, a heavy body, and a long neck and tail. But, wait a minute! What was that— that thing on the end of its tail?

Unlike other sauropods of its day, *Shunosaurus*'s tail ended with a bony lump. This hard lump was probably used like a club to bash predators who thought this big dinosaur would be an easy meal.

HEY! WATCH WHERE YOU'RE SWINGING THAT THING!

YEAH. DO I LOOK LIKE A BASEBALL?

UM, YOU SORTA DO.

47

STEGOSAURUS
Say it: STEG-oh-SORE-us

The thin plates standing on *Stegosaurus*'s back might have caught sunlight to help warm the animal. They might have been used to attract other *Stegosauruses*. Scientists aren't certain. They do believe that *Stegosaurus*'s spiked tail could have been a weapon. Tail fossils from *Stegosaurus* are often banged up—maybe from fighting. These strong beasts could have swung their tails with huge force.

Jumbled fossil footprints tell us that this animal might have traveled in groups—maybe family groups, like lions and elephants.

BONES FOUND IN: U.S. (COLORADO, UTAH, WYOMING)

ON THE MENU: PLANTS

SIZE: 26 TO 30 FEET (8 TO 9 METERS) LONG

BOY, LOTS OF DINOSAURS FOUGHT WITH THEIR TAILS.

YANGCHUSANOSAURUS
Say it: YANG-chew-san-oh-SORE-us

JURASSIC

During the Jurassic period, many plant-eaters lived in Asia, including the long-necked *Mamenchisaurus* a few pages back. Those plant-eating dinosaurs would have all been on *Yangchusanosaurus*'s menu. This dinosaur, with its tearing teeth and curved claws, could have chased those slower dinosaurs and torn them to pieces.

Yangchusanosaurus is another dinosaur discovered by accident—this time in the 1970s, when workers in China's Yellow River Valley were digging for a dam.

BONES FOUND IN: CHINA

ON THE MENU: MEAT

SIZE: 36 FEET (8.2 METERS) LONG

MAYBE WE SHOULD MOVE TO THE NEXT TIME PERIOD.

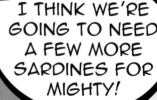

I THINK WE'RE GOING TO NEED A FEW MORE SARDINES FOR MIGHTY!

50

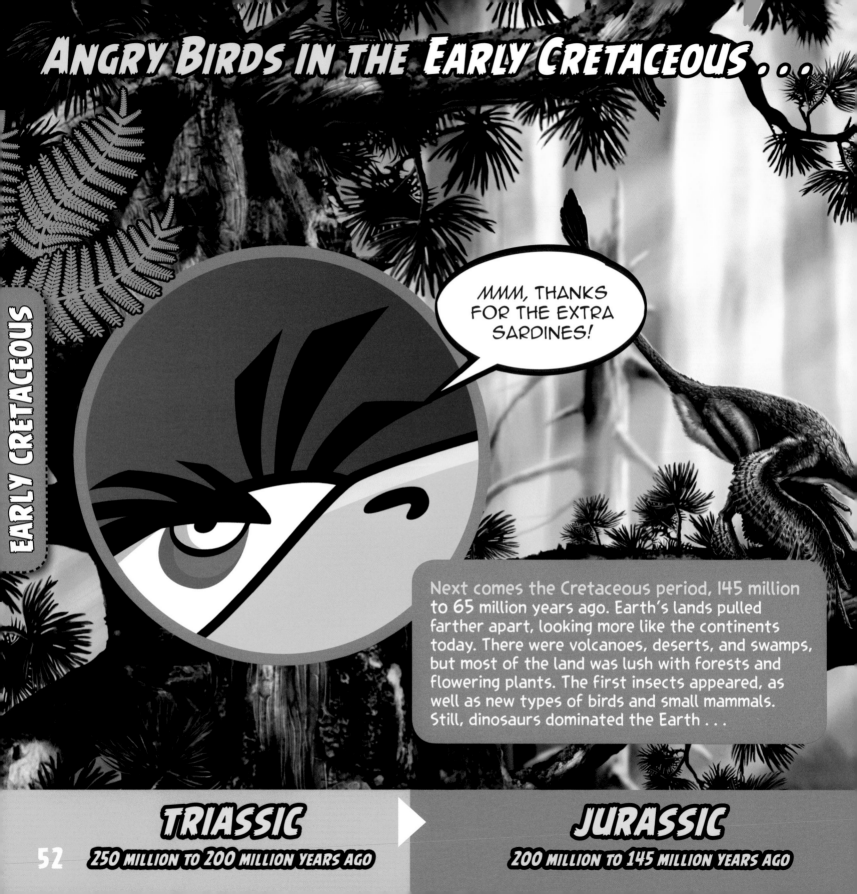

ANGRY BIRDS IN THE EARLY CRETACEOUS...

MMM, THANKS FOR THE EXTRA SARDINES!

Next comes the Cretaceous period, 145 million to 65 million years ago. Earth's lands pulled farther apart, looking more like the continents today. There were volcanoes, deserts, and swamps, but most of the land was lush with forests and flowering plants. The first insects appeared, as well as new types of birds and small mammals. Still, dinosaurs dominated the Earth . . .

TRIASSIC
250 MILLION TO 200 MILLION YEARS AGO

JURASSIC
200 MILLION TO 145 MILLION YEARS AGO

BARYONYX
Say it: BARE-ee-ON-icks

In 1983, a man in England saw a 12-inch (30.5-cm)-long, hooked claw sticking out of the side of a clay pit. Eventually, scientists found the rest of the fish-eating dinosaur's skeleton. How do they know it ate fish? They found fish scales and bones lying where its stomach would have been.

Baryonyx probably used its claws to help it scoop fish from rivers. And once a fish was locked in this dinosaur's crocodile-like jaws, there was no escape. Even the wiggliest fish had no chance against the 100 sharp teeth clamping it in place. *Chomp!*

MAKES YOU GLAD YOU'RE NOT A FISH, DOESN'T IT?

YOU CAN SAY THAT AGAIN.

MAKES YOU GLAD YOU'RE NOT A FISH, DOESN'T IT?

Not long ago, scientists learned that *Deinonychus* had feathers, just like some other dinosaurs—those known as birds!

DEINONYCHUS
Say it: die-NON-e-cuss

Deinonychus, about the size of a human, ran on its hind legs. It also had claws it could pull in—or retract—when they weren't needed. When it did use its claws, watch out! They were sharp and could slice terrible gashes into the skin of its prey. This animal may have hunted in packs, making it an especially scary predator.

LOOK! I'M A DEINONYCHUS. SEE MY CLAWS?

YOU DON'T HAVE CLAWS.

OR MAYBE HE DOES, AND HE'S HIDING THEM! NO FAIR! I WANT CLAWS, TOO!

BONES FOUND IN: U.S. (MONTANA, OKLAHOMA, UTAH, WYOMING)

ON THE MENU: MEAT

SIZE: 10 FEET (3 METERS) LONG

GASTONIA
Say it: gas-TONE-ee-ah

An enemy that tried to bite *Gastonia* might have found itself with a mouthful of broken teeth. That's because *Gastonia*'s skin was covered with pieces of bone—some flat, others pointy or even spiked. Double rows of spikes grew along the sides of its tail, too. *Gastonia* could have swung that tail at predators and cut their legs. For a predator to hurt this dinosaur, it would have had to flip *Gastonia* over to get at its soft belly.

BONES FOUND IN:
U.S. (UTAH)

ON THE MENU: PLANTS

SIZE: 13 TO 16 FEET (4 TO 5 METERS) LONG

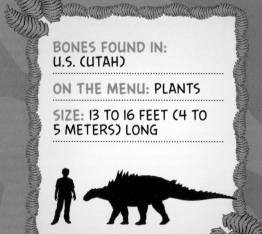

AWW, BET HE DIDN'T GET MANY HUGS.

IGUANODON
Say it: ig-WAN-oh-don

Iguanodon had thumb spikes that weren't really fingers but part of its wrist bone. It may have used these spikes to cut pieces from tasty-looking plants or even stab at attacking predators. This dinosaur could stand and walk on its hind legs to reach higher leaves or flowering plants. It had strong jaws and teeth, so it could eat plants that were tender or tough.

LET'S CALL THIS ONE SPIKE.

HOWDY, SPIKE!

BONES FOUND IN:
BELGIUM, ENGLAND,
GERMANY

ON THE MENU: PLANTS

SIZE: 33 FEET (10 METERS)
LONG

The *Iguanodon*
bones discovered
in southern England
in 1822 were the
first real proof of
dinosaurs found by
humans.

BONES FOUND IN: CHINA

ON THE MENU: MEAT

SIZE: 22 INCHES
(56 CENTIMETERS) LONG

MICRORAPTOR
Say it: MY-crow-RAP-tore

Bird-like *Microraptor* had feathered wings attached to its long arms, but its back legs were feathered, too! *Microraptor* had sharp claws it probably used to hang on to tree trunks or pull itself higher. Its strange feathery tail might have helped it steer while gliding through the forest.

OOH, I WANT TO GLIDE LIKE THAT!

YOU'D NEED LONGER TAIL FEATHERS.

OR, YOU KNOW, ACTUAL WINGS.

BONES FOUND IN:
AUSTRALIA

ON THE MENU: PLANTS

SIZE: 24 FEET (7.3 METERS)
LONG

MUTTABURRASAURUS
Say it: mutt-ah-BUHR-ah-SORE-us

Muttaburrasaurus had a large bump on its face, near its nose. Nobody knows why. Did the bump improve this dinosaur's sense of smell? Make its calls sound louder? Or was it just to make the dinosaur look more attractive to others like itself? We can only guess.

Scientists also have to guess what the *Muttaburrasaurus*'s arms looked like. That's because, even though skeletons of this animal have been discovered in Australia, no arm bones have yet been found.

I'LL SAY!

Scientists wonder: Did *Muttaburrasaurus* have thumb spikes? Nobody will know until arm bones turn up.

WOW, NOW THAT'S A MOSQUITO BITE!

PSITTACOSAURUS

Say it: SIT-ah-co-SORE-us

Scientists think *Psittacosaurus*'s parrot-like beak was covered in keratin, like human fingernails. This animal probably ran on two legs near lakeshores, where plants were plentiful, and used its tough beak like powerful scissors to bite off low branches, *snip-snip-snip*.

Often, only pieces of a dinosaur's skeleton are found. When that happens, scientists compare those few bones to the skeletons of similar animals, then make best guesses about how a dinosaur's body was shaped. But scientists don't have to guess what *Psittacosaurus* looked like. More than 400 of its skeletons have been found!

EITHER THAT, OR A REALLY BAD HAIRCUT.

THIS ONE'S GOT STICKY-UP FEATHERS ON ITS TAIL!

BONES FOUND IN:
CHINA, MONGOLIA,
THAILAND

ON THE MENU: PLANTS

SIZE: 5.6 FEET
(1.7 METERS) LONG

REBBACHISAURUS
Say it: re-BASH-eh-SORE-us

EARLY CRETACEOUS

Parts of this *lonnnnng* dinosaur's backbone have been found in Africa and Spain. By comparing them to the bones of other dinosaurs, scientists realized that *Rebbachisaurus* was a sauropod. Unlike other dinosaurs, *Rebbachisaurus* had a ridge on top of its back. Scientists think this ridge may have helped the animal warm up or cool down more quickly.

HA-HA! BASH PIGS!

IT SOUNDS LIKE *BASH*!

I LIKE THIS NAME: *REBBACHISAURUS.*

The giant *Rebbachisaurus* lived in the forest.

68

BONES FOUND IN:
MOROCCO, NIGER, SPAIN,
TUNISIA

ON THE MENU: PLANTS

SIZE: 68 FEET
(20.7 METERS) LONG

SCANSORIOPTERYX

Say it: SCAN-sore-ee-OP-tore-icks

Scansoriopteryx's long toes and strong claws tell scientists it was a tree-climber. It also had a stiff tail that could have helped this little dinosaur stay propped upright against a trunk as it poked for insects, like today's woodpeckers.

Scansoriopteryx couldn't fly, but it probably liked spending time high in trees, away from bigger creatures. Bigger, hungry creatures.

FOR SOME REASON, I LIKE THIS GUY.

IT'S THE FEATHERS. GOTTA BE THE FEATHERS.

71

SPINOSAURUS
Say it: SPINE-oh-SORE-us

EARLY CRETACEOUS

Think *Tyrannosaurus rex* was the scariest dinosaur? Meet *Spinosaurus*. This meat-eater was longer than *T. rex* but lighter on its feet and probably just as ferocious. *Spinosaurus* means "spined lizard." The spines on its back were probably covered with skin and could be raised over five feet (1.5 m) into the air.

Spinosaurus spent its days along waterways, stepping through the shallows, dunking its crocodile-like head into the water to snatch unlucky fish. But other dinosaurs were also on its menu. And none of them would have wanted to tangle with this beast.

...AND INTRODUCE HIM TO THE PIGS!

TOO BAD WE CAN'T TAKE HIM HOME...

UTAHRAPTOR
Say it: YOO-tah-RAP-tore

Utahraptor was big—and fast—with ripping teeth and powerful legs that made jumping and kicking easy. Each of its feet had one especially horrible claw, an eight-inch (20-cm)-long slicer that flexed forward as *Utahraptor* kicked.

A thick tail helped this dinosaur keep its balance, so it could swing those feet way out to slash the air—and any other dinosaur, small or large, unlucky enough to get in its way. When this dinosaur kicked, the best thing to do was scram!

WOULD YOU LOOK AT THOSE TOENAILS?

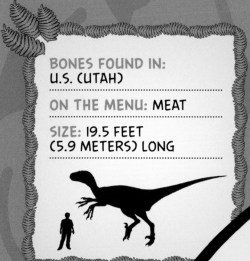

BONES FOUND IN:
U.S. (UTAH)

ON THE MENU: MEAT

SIZE: 19.5 FEET
(5.9 METERS) LONG

74

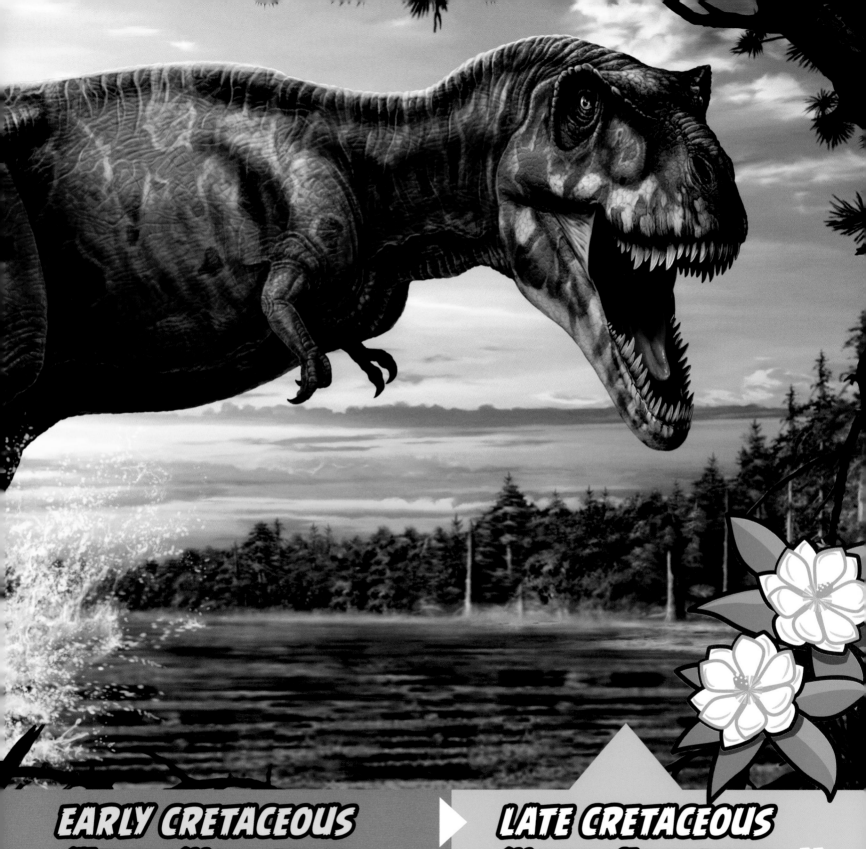

ANKYLOSAURUS
Say it: AN-kye-loh-SORE-us

Ankylosaurus didn't move very fast. But predators would have had to be really hungry to mess with this dinosaur. It had super-tough, tooth-chipping skin, and a tail built for more than wagging. Like a few other dinosaurs, *Ankylosaurus*'s powerful tail ended in a heavy club of skin-covered bones. *Ankylosaurus* couldn't swing its tail very far sideways, but one well-aimed hit—*wham!*—could have broken the bones of an enemy.

With its short legs and stiff back, this dinosaur probably couldn't lift its head very far. Good thing it liked to eat grasses and other low-growing plants, snipping sprouts with its small, leaf-shaped teeth as it wandered along.

I'D LIKE A TAIL LIKE THAT.

BONES FOUND IN: U.S. (MONTANA) AND CANADA (ALBERTA)

ON THE MENU: PLANTS

SIZE: 25 TO 35 FEET (7.5 TO 10.7 METERS) LONG

ARGENTINOSAURUS
Say it: ahr-gen-TEEN-uh-SORE-us

A farmer in Argentina saw something odd sticking out of the ground. He thought it was a piece of ancient wood. But it wasn't wood. It was the gigantic shinbone of a dinosaur! This dinosaur was not yet known to scientists. Only a dozen of this dinosaur's bones are known, but those were enough to help scientists figure out what the creature looked like. This new dinosaur, soon named *Argentinosaurus*, was ENORMOUS, weighing as much as 20 elephants, and is the largest land animal that ever lived . . . so far.

THAT'S YOUR CHIN. YOUR SHIN IS THE FRONT OF YOUR LEG BELOW THE KNEE.

A SHINBONE? I HAVE ONE OF THOSE BELOW MY BEAK.

BONES FOUND IN: ARGENTINA

ON THE MENU: PLANTS

SIZE: 130 TO 140 FEET (40 TO 42 METERS) LONG

Fossils are the remains of animals or plants that once lived on Earth. These might be bones, teeth, leaves, shells, or even an animal's poop. Fossils can also be imprints left in stone.

BONES FOUND IN:
U.S. (ALASKA, MONTANA,
NEW JERSEY, WYOMING)
AND CANADA (ALBERTA)

ON THE MENU: PLANTS

SIZE: 42 FEET (12.8
METERS) LONG

EDMONTOSAURUS
Say it: ed-MON-toh-SORE-us

Edmontosaurus lived in the same time and neighborhood as *Tyrannosaurus rex*. For better protection from that meat-eater, *Edmontosaurus*, a plant-eater, lived in large herds. The herds migrated with the seasons, always searching for the best food.

Edmontosaurus had a beaked mouth with hundreds of small, diamond-shaped teeth. It could move its jaws side to side to grind plants before swallowing. On its nose was a floppy skin pouch. The animal could fill it with air, then honk the air out like a noisy frog.

I CAN HONK, TOO. *AWNK! AWNK! AWNK!*

YOU SOUND LIKE A GOOSE.

83

GIGANOTOSAURUS
Say it: JYE-ga-NO-toe-SORE-us

Only one skeleton of *Giganotosaurus* has been found. But that was enough to tell us that this beast was a frightening hunter. It was longer and heavier than *Tyrannosaurus rex,* and lighter than *Spinosaurus.* Throw in its razor-sharp teeth, and you get an animal so dangerous that nobody but its mother could have been happy to see it coming.

EVEN HIS NAME SOUNDS BIG: GIGANOTOSAURUS!

BONES FOUND IN:
ARGENTINA

ON THE MENU: MEAT

SIZE: 45 FEET (13.7 METERS) LONG

OVIRAPTOR
Say it: OH-vih-RAP-tore

YEAH, AN EGG PROTECTOR.

This dinosaur's name means "egg thief." Why? Because scientists first found its bones near a nest of eggs that they believed belonged to another dinosaur. *Hmm,* thought the scientists. *The* Oviraptor *must have been stealing those eggs!*

A scientific guess like that is called a *hypothesis.*

Many years later, scientists found another *Oviraptor* skeleton—atop a nest of the same kind of eggs. That's when they knew the old hypothesis was wrong. That first *Oviraptor* wasn't *stealing* some other dinosaur's eggs. It was *protecting* its own! *Oops.*

MY NEW FAVORITE DINOSAUR.

PACHYCEPHALOSAURUS
Say it: pack-ee-SEF-ah-lo-SORE-us

Skulls found from this beast measure nine inches (22.9 cm) thick! No wonder its name means "thick-headed lizard." *Pachycephalosaurus* must have used that thick head for something besides thinking. Scientists believe these dinosaurs head-butted each other in the side, sometimes knocking another *Pachycephalosaurus* off its feet. These head-butts might have meant, "Get out of my territory!" or "Go away. This is mine!"

HEE, HEE.

PREPARE TO BE HEAD-BUTTED!

GO AHEAD. I'LL JUST SPIN AWAY.

SOUNDS PAINFUL!

BONES FOUND IN:
U.S. (MONTANA, SOUTH
DAKOTA, WYOMING)
AND MONGOLIA

ON THE MENU: PLANTS

SIZE: 15 FEET (4.6 METERS)
LONG

BONES FOUND IN: EGYPT

ON THE MENU: PLANTS

SIZE: 78 TO 100 FEET (24 TO 30 METERS) LONG

PARALITITAN
Say it: pah-ral-e-TIE-tan

In the time of dinosaurs, the Sahara desert was a shallow ocean. At the edge of this ocean, in a mangrove swamp, lived one of the largest dinosaurs, *Paralititan*. You want big? Its upper arm bone was six feet (1.8 m) long!

Only a few bones and bone pieces from one of these animals have been found so far, but scientists think there could be many more dinosaurs buried in the Sahara, just waiting to be discovered.

ME, THREE!

I'M GOING TO DISCOVER A DINOSAUR SOMEDAY.

ME, TOO!

PARASAUROLOPHUS
Say it: PAR-ah-saw-RAH-loh-fuss

Parasaurolophus had a bony tube, or crest, on top of its head that once stumped scientists. Was it used to help the animal breathe underwater? Did it make smelling easier for *Parasaurolophus* or keep its brain cool? None of those ideas made much sense.

Now scientists believe that the tube was a noisemaker. The inside had hollow airways, sort of like a trombone. It connected the animal's nose with the back of its throat. *Parasaurolophus* could make different sounds through the tube to signal things like, "Hey, guys, I'm over here!" or "RUN!" to others in its herd.

WHA-? I WANT ONE OF THOSE!

ME, TOO. WE COULD BLAST REALLY LOUD!

BONES FOUND IN:
U.S. (NEW MEXICO)

ON THE MENU: PLANTS

SIZE: 28 FEET (8.5
METERS) LONG

PENTACERATOPS
Say it: PEN-ta-SER-ah-tops

When a word begins with "penta," it means five of something. *Pentaceratops* got its name because of the five horns growing out of its head. And what a head—it was 9.8 feet (3 m) long! No other land animal, before or since, has had such a massive head.

Pentaceratops's horns make it look like one tough customer, but guess what? The horns were actually too thin for fighting. They would have broken. Scientists think the horns may have just been for decoration.

One thing's for sure: The horns, along with the jaggedy frill stretching high over its head, would have made the *Pentaceratops* stand out in any crowd.

HEY, I ONLY SEE THREE HORNS!

LOOK CLOSER. TWO MORE STICK OUT FROM ITS CHEEKS.

Some dinosaurs, like *Pentaceratops*, look like they're wearing a high collar. This is actually skin-covered bone growing up from the back of their skulls. It is called a frill.

PROTOCERATOPS
Say it: PRO-toh-SERR-ah-tops

Protoceratops lived in Asia's Gobi desert. It was the size of a large dog and probably lived in herds. Scientists know this plant-eater was prey for the ferocious *Velociraptor.* How can they be sure? Because they once found a *Protoceratops* fossil with a *Velociraptor* skeleton wrapped around it! The two may have been fighting near a high sand dune that caved in and buried them.

YOU GOT IT.

REMIND ME NOT TO FIGHT THE PIGS NEAR SAND DUNES.

BONES FOUND IN: MONGOLIA

ON THE MENU: PLANTS

SIZE: 6 FEET (1.8 METERS) LONG

TARCHIA
Say it: TAHR-key-ah

BET HE COULD TAKE ON A BULLDOZER.

Tarchia looks frightful, but it was actually a plant-eater. This heavyweight tipped the scales at nearly 10,000 pounds (4,536 kg). Its wide head tells us that it had a large brain to match. Covering the head were bony lumps, and spikes that stuck out in all directions.

Tarchia's tough, armored skin was its best protection. But it also had a clubbed tail it may have used against predators that got too close. *Tarchia* lived in a dry area and grazed on short plants growing near lakes and streams.

BONES FOUND IN: MONGOLIA

ON THE MENU: PLANTS

SIZE: 26 TO 28 FEET (8 TO 8.5 METERS) LONG

THERIZINOSAURUS
Say it: THERE-ih-ZIN-oh-SORE-us

Not much is known about *Therizinosaurus*. All that has been found of it are a few arm and leg bones and some BIG, three-foot (1-m)-long claws. Scientists think it was a plant-eater. But what about those claws? Were they used to pull branches closer to its mouth? Did they strip bark from trees? Or maybe *Therizinosaurus* liked eating ants and beetles. Maybe it used its claws to scrape in the dirt to find them. We just don't know.

What we do know is that no other dinosaur yet discovered had claws as large as these.

HE REALLY NEEDS TO TRIM THOSE FINGERNAILS!

CAREFUL, BUDDY. DON'T POKE YOURSELF IN THE EYE!

What do you think those claws might have been used for?

BONES FOUND IN: CHINA AND MONGOLIA

ON THE MENU: PLANTS AND INSECTS

SIZE: 36 FEET (11 METERS) LONG

TRICERATOPS
Say it: tri-SERR-eh-tops

Triceratops means "three-horned face." And what horns! The ones above this dinosaur's eyes were three feet (1 m) long! *Triceratops* was a slow-moving plant-eater. It wandered along, its giant head to the ground, nipping low-growing plants with its beak-like mouth. Inside its cheeks, 800 little chewing teeth chomped food to bits.

But sometimes, *Triceratops* had to defend itself from hungry meat-eaters like *Tyrannosaurus rex*. Luckily, it had those horns and a tough frill to protect its neck.

800 TEETH?!

WOW.

BONES FOUND IN: WESTERN CANADA AND WESTERN U.S.

ON THE MENU: PLANTS

SIZE: 25 FEET (7.6 METERS) LONG

TROODON
Say it: TRO-oh-don

BONES FOUND IN: U.S. (ALASKA, MONTANA, WYOMING) AND CANADA (ALBERTA)

ON THE MENU: MEAT

SIZE: 6.5 FEET (2 METERS) LONG

LATE CRETACEOUS

*T*roodon had big eyes that faced forward. That tells us it was a good hunter, maybe even at night. It may have been the smartest of all dinosaurs, too. How do we know? Because its golf-ball-size brain was large for the size of its head.

In *Troodon's* mouth were different-shaped teeth, which means it ate different kinds of food. It was a known meat-eater, so lizards and small mammals were probably its favorite prey. But if *Troodon* hunted in packs, putting its good eyesight, brainy mind, and scary claws to work, it could have easily brought down much larger animals.

AWK! HE LOOKS ANGRY.

YOU SAY THAT LIKE IT'S A BAD THING.

TSINTAOSAURUS
Say it: sin-tau-SORE-us

Nobody believed the scientist who announced this animal's discovery. Oh, they believed he'd found a new kind of dinosaur. But that head spike? Nah, that was just too weird to be true. Everyone thought he must have made a mistake. Then another skeleton was found—with the same odd head spike—and scientists knew it was real.

Tsintaosaurus had a duck-like bill. Inside, hundreds of tiny teeth ground up whatever the dinosaur ate, even tough food like pinecones. If the teeth wore down, new ones grew in.

BONES FOUND IN: CHINA

ON THE MENU: PLANTS

SIZE: 33 FEET (10 METERS) LONG

I THINK THEY MIGHT BE SIGNALING SPACE!

106

Scientists wonder: What was that spike used for? What do you think?

107

WHAT TEENY ARMS!

Scientists wonder: Were *T. rex* and other dinosaurs warm-blooded, like mammals and birds? Or cold-blooded, like reptiles?

108

TYRANNOSAURUS REX
Say it: tye-RAN-oh-SORE-us rex

Tyrannosaurus rex had tiny, useless arms—it's true. But *T. rex*'s humongous mouth made it one of the scariest animals that ever lived. Scientists think those killer jaws—studded with banana-size teeth—could tear off 500 pounds (227 kg) of meat in each bite and crunch right through any bones that got in the way. Because it was so heavy, *T. rex* probably couldn't run, but it could walk fast—*thump, thump, thump*—with long strides that let it easily overtake its prey.

YEAH. BET HE COULDN'T EVEN DO A PULL-UP.

LOOK WHO'S TALKING!

BONES FOUND IN: U.S. (COLORADO, MONTANA, NEW MEXICO, SOUTH DAKOTA, WYOMING) AND CANADA (ALBERTA AND SASKATCHEWAN)

ON THE MENU: MEAT

SIZE: 40 FEET (12 METERS) LONG

VELOCIRAPTOR
Say it: veh-LOSS-ih-RAP-tore

This brainy dino wasn't huge, but it had a mouthful of sharp teeth and was extremely quick on its feet. It had a large, hooked claw on each hand and foot that could grab and kill quickly. A pack hunter, *Velociraptor* probably chased down smaller animals.

But larger animals would have had to watch out for *Velociraptor*, too. *Protoceratops* skeletons have been found tangled with *Velociraptor* skeletons, showing us that these dinosaurs were fighting when they died.

BONES FOUND IN: MONGOLIA

ON THE MENU: MEAT

SIZE: 6.5 FEET (2 METERS) LONG

SO THIS GUY IS RELATED TO US?!

MAKES SENSE.

YEAH. HE SEEMS REALLY, REALLY ANGRY.

TAKE A LOOK.
I DECIDED TO MAKE
A SCRAPBOOK OF
WHAT WE LEARNED
ABOUT DINOSAURS.

TRIASSIC:

At the beginning of the Triassic period, all of Earth's land was connected. Scientists believe that the climate was hot and dry, although it could have been as varied as today's climate. There were low-growing plants, but probably no tall trees or ice—not even at the North or South Poles. The biggest animals alive were no bigger than pigs. By the end of the Triassic, both plants and animals were increasing in size.

How are fossils created? After lying buried under heavy layers of sand or mud for thousands of years, animal bones, claws, or teeth—as well as plants— become fossilized as, over time, living matter is replaced by minerals.

How do scientists determine a fossil's age? Dating the rock surrounding a fossil in a process called radio-metric age dating gives scientists an idea of when an animal or plant lived.

JURASSIC:

During the Jurassic period, Earth's landmasses began to pull apart. Seas rose higher, and flooding was common. There were deserts, yes, but other lands were green and growing. The first birds appeared. Dinosaurs grew to enormous sizes, and there were more and different kinds of them.

CRETACEOUS:

The Cretaceous period was a time of great change. Earth's lands pulled farther apart, looking more like the continents we know today. Volcanoes were common. There were deserts and swamps, but most of the land was lush with forests and flowering plants. The first insects appeared, as well as new types of birds and small mammals. Still, dinosaurs dominated the Earth.

DINOSAUR FOSSIL MAP

Nearly 1,000 kinds of dinosaurs have been discovered so far. But scientists think there are many more yet to be found. Remember, most new dinosaurs are found by amateurs—people who are not trained scientists. People like you.

Map labels:
Alaska (U.S.)
Canada
Alberta → ← Saskatchewan
North America
Montana → North Dakota
← Wyoming
Utah → ← Colorado
← New Jersey
Arizona → ← Oklahoma
New Mexico
United States
Atlantic Ocean
United Kingdom
Ger
Belgium
Portugal Spa
Morocco
Tuni
Ni
A
South America
Argentina

NORTH AMERICA–CANADA

Ankylosaurus—Alberta
Edmontosaurus—Alberta
Parasaurolophus—
Alberta

Triceratops—Alberta, Saskatchewan
Troodon—Alberta, Saskatchewan
Tyrannosaurus rex—Alberta, Saskatchewan

NORTH AMERICA–UNITED STATES*

Allosaurus—
CO, MT, UT, WY
Ankylosaurus—MT
Apatosaurus—
CO, OK, UT, WY
Brachiosaurus—CO
Camptosaurus—
CO, ND, UT, WY
Coelophysis— AZ, NM
Deinonychus—
MT, OK, UT, WY
Diplodocus—
CO, MT, UT, WY
Edmontosaurus—
AK, MT, NJ, WY
Gastonia—UT

Pachycephalosaurus—
MT, SD, WY
Parasaurolophus—
NM, UT
Pentaceratops—NM
Scutellosaurus—AZ
Stegosaurus—
CO, UT, WY
Triceratops—CO, MT, SD, WY
Troodon—AK, MT, WY
Tyrannosaurus rex—
CO, MT, NM, SD, WY
Utahraptor—UT

*States are abbreviated (see page 127 for key)

SOUTH AMERICA–ARGENTINA

Argentinosaurus
Eoraptor
Giganotosaurus
Herrerasaurus
Lessemsaurus
Riojasaurus

116

Arctic Ocean

Archaeopteryx–Germany
Baryonyx–England (UK), Spain
Camptosaurus–England
Iguanodon–England, Belgium, Germany
Lourinhanosaurus–Portugal
Plateosaurus–northern and central
Rebbachisaurus–Spain

Europe

Asia

Mongolia

China

Egypt

Thailand

Pacific Ocean

Indian Ocean

ica

Africa

Antarctica

Australia

ASIA
Mamenchisaurus–China
Microraptor–China
Oviraptor–China, Mongolia
Pachycephalosaurus–Mongolia
Protoceratops–Mongolia
Psittacosaurus– China, Mongolia, Thailand
Scansoriopteryx–China
Shunosaurus–China
Tarchia–Mongolia
Therizinosaurus–China, Mongolia
Tsintaosaurus–China
Velociraptor–Mongolia
Yangchusanosaurus–China

AFRICA
Baryonyx–Niger
Brachiosaurus
Paralititan–Egypt
Rebbachisaurus–Morocco, Niger, Tunisia
Spinosaurus–Morocco, Egypt

ANTARCTICA
Cryolophosaurus

AUSTRALIA
Muttaburrasaurus

117

QUIZ TIME!

1. Most dinosaurs have long names with lots of different letters. How many times does the letter **A** appear in **PACHYCEPHALOSAURUS?** Point to each **A** as you count aloud.

QUIZ TIME!

2. A *Triceratops* has **3 eggs** and another has **2 eggs**. How many eggs are there all together?

3 + 2 = ?

A. 4   B. 5   C. 7

PARENT TIP: Encourage your child to create simple number sentences on his own using items found around the home or, at mealtimes, with segments of fruit, vegetables, or slices of pizza.

3. Trace the paths that will take each dinosaur back to its home.

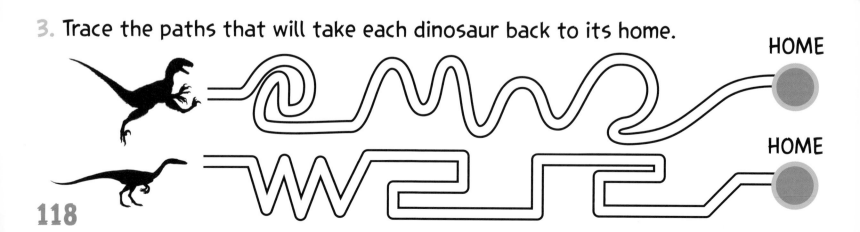

HOME

HOME

4. Which dinosaur has more spikes on its head, the *Triceratops* or the *Pentaceratops*?

TRICERATOPS

PENTACERATOPS

5. *Apatosaurus* may have traveled in herds. Grab a piece of paper and write a story about a small dinosaur trying to keep up with this group. *Is he excited or worried? Where is the herd going, and what will he do when they get there?*

PARENT TIP: Make the story into a book by folding four sheets of copier paper in half, then writing your child's story, a little on each page. Allow her to illustrate.

6. Point to the shape below that will complete each dinosaur outline.

1.

2.

3.

a.

b.

c.

7. Can you unscramble the words below to find some dinosaur-related words?

a. FLIRL   b. STECR   c. HETET   d. EBNOS

__ __ __ __ __   __ __ __ __ __   __ __ __ __ __   __ __ __ __ __

8. Which dinosaur footprint below is the smallest? Which is the largest?

9. On a piece of paper, draw a picture of your favorite dinosaur from this book. Color its head red, its body green, and its legs and tail purple.

10. Which two dinosaurs belong to the same group?

PARENT TIP: *Look for other opportunities to teach your child about same/different by grouping toys, items of clothing, or even snacks.*

RIOJASAURUS

LESSEMSAURUS

MICRORAPTOR

BONUS ACTIVITIES

Short of traveling back in time, the best way to learn about dinosaurs is to visit a natural history museum to see their fossils and bones. But you can have dinosaur fun at home, too. Here are additional activities you and your child can share to take his or her experiences beyond the pages of this book.

DINO SIGHT

Some dinosaurs had forward-facing eyes. Others had eyes located on the sides of their heads. Hold your hands in front your eyes so that you cannot see straight ahead, only to the side. Try walking around. Would dinosaurs that saw like this be good hunters? Discuss why or why not.

DINO WATCHING

How are birds like—or different from—their dinosaur relatives? Grab a pad and pencil and head outside. Study birds in your backyard or neighborhood. How many toes do birds have? What kind of footprints do they leave behind as they hop or walk? How do birds capture prey, with their feet or with their beaks? Are their eyes on the sides of their heads, or are they forward-facing?

DINOSAUR HIDE AND SEEK

Hide a toy dinosaur. Have your child search for the dinosaur, letting her know when she is hot (close) or cold (farther away). Alternative: You might also hide a plastic "dinosaur" egg with a treat inside.

DINO DIG

Draw a big dinosaur on a sheet of poster board then cut it out. Cut this dino shape into puzzle pieces. Hide the pieces around the yard and ask your child to search for them, then reconstruct the dinosaur. This can be done on a smaller scale, indoors, with pieces hidden in a shallow dish of dry beans or rice.

DINO MEMORY MATCH

Make two identical sets of dinosaur cards. Mix up the cards, then place them facedown on a table or the floor. Take turns selecting two cards at a time. If they match, set aside. If not, flip them over again and let the next player take a turn. Play until all the pictures are matched.

DINO DASH

Talk about different ways dinosaurs moved, then move like them. Walk slowly like *Stegosaurus*. Jump and kick like *Deinonychus*. Shuffle along heavily like *Brachiosaurus*. Roll up a sock and stuff it into the end of another long sock. Pin it at the back of your child's waistband like a tail. Can he swing it like *Ankylosaurus?*

MAKE A DINOSAUR EGG

Blow up a balloon. Make a runny paste by mixing flour and water in a bowl. Tear newspaper into strips. Dip in paste, remove excess, then place the strips on the balloon. Overlap the strips until the balloon is covered. Apply three or four layers, then allow to dry. Once dry, the "dinosaur egg" can be painted. Were dino eggs white or brown or brightly colored? Were they striped or spotted? Nobody knows for sure, so anything goes.

DINO BONES

Using the same technique as the craft above, make dinosaur bones by taping balls of scrunched newspaper to the ends of an empty toilet paper or paper towel tube. Cover with newspaper strips dipped in paste. When dry, paint to look like a bone.

HOW BIG IS BIG?

Mark a starting spot in a grassy, open area. Using a measuring tape, information from this book, and flags, mark various dinosaur lengths to illustrate how tremendous the dinosaurs were.

BONUS ACTIVITIES

SALT DOUGH FOSSILS

Explain to your child that fossils are made over thousands of years. Help her understand the concept by making salt dough fossils. *Salt dough:* In a large bowl, mix 2 cups of flour and I cup of salt. Slowly add I cup of water. Knead 5 minutes. To create fossil imprints, press dinosaur toys, coins, leaves, sticks, or your child's own hands or feet into the dough. If your child would like to preserve her fossils, let air dry or dry in a 200° oven for an hour or more, depending on thickness of dough. May be painted after dry.

SCULPT-A-DINO

With salt dough, make a dinosaur sculpture. When dough is dry, paint as desired.

DINO DINING

Some dinosaurs ate plants. Others were meat-eaters. Whichever they preferred, most could not use their hands to eat, only their mouths. What was that like? To find out, put a variety of your child's favorite sliced fruits, melons, or vegetables on a plate. Allow him to try eating like a dino—with no hands. Would he want to eat this way all of the time? Why or why not?

DINO FOOTPRINT

The *Apatosaurus* had huge feet, about 36 inches long and 42 inches wide. Use sidewalk chalk to draw a three-toed dinosaur footprint on your sidewalk or driveway to those dimensions. Ask your child to guess how many of her own footprints would fit inside. Now trace your child's footprint inside the dino print as many times as it will fit. Was her guess close? Help your child imagine how big an animal would have to be to have feet this gigantic.

BIG DINO FEET

Make dino feet out of empty tissue boxes (the type with a slotted top). If desired, color the boxes and draw claws with a marker to look more realistic. Stomp around like a dinosaur.

DINO SOUNDS

We aren't sure what dinosaurs sounded like, but we know they didn't all sound alike. Some growled or grunted, others probably honked or snorted or trumpeted or even tweeted. Go through this book, demonstrating how you think each dinosaur may have sounded.

MEASURING FUN

Paralititan's upper arm bone was nearly six feet (1.8 m) long! Have your child measure his own upper arm bone and compare it to that of *Paralititan.*

INVENT A NEW DINOSAUR

Many dinosaurs had features that made them stand out from all the rest: the bony back plates of *Stegosaurus,* the horns of *Pentaceratops,* the strange spike of *Tsintaosaurus.* Have your child draw and color a picture of a dinosaur with a different-from-everybody-else feature. Stress that scientists are finding new dinosaur species every year.

DEM BONES

Using many different pasta shapes, construct a dinosaur skeleton by gluing the pasta on a sheet of construction paper. Look at the pictures in this book for inspiration.

GLOSSARY

Not sure what all those big words mean? Check out the definitions of some of the harder words right here.

ANTARCTICA: very cold, mostly ice-covered land at the bottom of the Earth

CREST: bony, flesh-covered areas on a dinosaur's face or head

DINOSAUR: a reptile that lived millions of years ago

EARLY CRETACEOUS: the time period 145 million to 100 million years ago

FOSSIL: the remains (bones turned to stone) or impressions of animals or plants that lived millions of years ago

FRILL: skin-covered bone growing up from the back of a dinosaur's skull

GASTROLITHS: stones an animal swallows to help it digest food in its stomach

HYPOTHESIS: scientific guess

JURASSIC: the time period 200 million to 145 million years ago

KERATIN: what hair, feathers, fingernails, claws, and horns are made from

LATE CRETACEOUS: the time period 100 million to 65 million years ago

MANGROVE:
a tree growing in coastal swamps that has tangled, above-ground roots

PREDATOR:
an animal that hunts others for food

PREY:
an animal that is hunted by other animals

RADIOMETRIC AGE DATING:
a process to date the rock surrounding a fossil that gives scientists an idea of when an animal or plant lived

SAUROPOD:
very large, four-legged plant-eating dinosaur with a long neck and tail, small head, and thick body

SCUTES:
bony, protective plates; part of an animal's skin

SKELETON:
framework of bone in an animal's body

TRIASSIC:
the time period 250 million to 200 million years ago

INDEX

Boldface indicates illustrations.

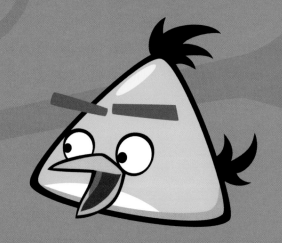

STATE ABBREVIATIONS KEY

Alabama	AL	Montana	MT
Alaska	AK	Nebraska	NE
Arizona	AZ	Nevada	NV
Arkansas	AR	New Hampshire	NH
California	CA	New Jersey	NJ
Colorado	CO	New Mexico	NM
Connecticut	CT	New York	NY
Delaware	DE	North Carolina	NC
Florida	FL	North Dakota	ND
Georgia	GA	Ohio	OH
Hawaii	HI	Oklahoma	OK
Idaho	ID	Oregon	OR
Illinois	IL	Pennsylvania	PA
Indiana	IN	Rhode Island	RI
Iowa	IA	South Carolina	SC
Kansas	KS	South Dakota	SD
Kentucky	KY	Tennessee	TN
Louisiana	LA	Texas	TX
Maine	ME	Utah	UT
Maryland	MD	Vermont	VT
Massachusetts	MA	Virginia	VA
Michigan	MI	Washington	WA
Minnesota	MN	West Virginia	WV
Mississippi	MS	Wisconsin	WI
Missouri	MO	Wyoming	WY

All dinosaur artwork by Franco Tempesta. Angry Birds in caveman costumes and scenes by Dan Sipple. Photo, p. 86, by Joyce Photographics/Photo Researchers, Inc.

Published by the National Geographic Society
John M. Fahey, Chairman of the Board and Chief Executive Officer
Declan Moore, Executive Vice President; President, Publishing and Travel
Melina Gerosa Bellows, Executive Vice President; Chief Creative Officer, Books, Kids, and Family

Prepared by the Book Division
Hector Sierra, Senior Vice President and General Manager
Nancy Laties Feresten, Senior Vice President, Kids Publishing and Media
Jennifer Emmett, Vice President, Editorial Director, Children's Books
Eva Absher-Schantz, Design Director, Kids Publishing and Media
Jay Sumner, Director of Photography, Kids Publishing and Media
R. Gary Colbert, Production Director
Jennifer A. Thornton, Director of Managing Editorial

Staff for This Book
Rebecca Baines, Editor
Susan Kehnemui Donnelly, Project Editor
Lori Epstein, Senior Illustrations Editor
Nicole Lazarus, Designer
Franco Tempesta, Dinosaur Illustrator
Dan Sipple, Illustrator
Hillary Moloney, Illustrations Assistant
Carl Mehler, Director of Maps
Ariane Szu-Tu, Editorial Assistant
Callie Broaddus, Design Production Assistant
Grace Hill, Michael O'Connor, Associate Managing Editors
Joan Gossett, Production Editor
Lewis R. Bassford, Production Manager
Susan Borke, Legal and Business Affairs

Rovio Entertainment Ltd.
Sanna Lukander, Vice President of Book Publishing
Mari Elomäki, Project Editor
Pekka Laine, Project Editor
Jan Schulte-Tigges, Art Director

Manufacturing and Quality Management
Phillip L. Schlosser, Senior Vice President
Chris Brown, Vice President, NG Book Manufacturing
George Bounelis, Vice President, Production Services
Nicole Elliott, Manager
Rachel Faulise, Manager
Robert L. Barr, Manager

THAT'S A LOT OF NAMES!